Dear Parent:

Congratulations! Your child is taking the first steps on an exciting journey. The destination? Independent reading!

STEP INTO READING® will help your child get there. The program offers books at five levels that accompany children from their first attempts at reading to reading success. Each step includes fun stories, fiction and nonfiction, and colorful art. There are also Step into Reading Sticker Books, Step into Reading Math Readers, and Step into Reading Phonics Readers—a complete literacy program with something to interest every child.

Learning to Read, Step by Step!

Ready to Read Preschool–Kindergarten
• big type and easy words • rhyme and rhythm • picture clues
For children who know the alphabet and are eager to begin reading.

Reading with Help Preschool–Grade 1
• basic vocabulary • short sentences • simple stories
For children who recognize familiar words and sound out new words with help.

Reading on Your Own Grades 1–3
• engaging characters • easy-to-follow plots • popular topics
For children who are ready to read on their own.

Reading Paragraphs Grades 2–3
• challenging vocabulary • short paragraphs • exciting stories
For newly independent readers who read simple sentences with confidence.

Ready for Chapters Grades 2–4
• chapters • longer paragraphs • full-color art
For children who want to take the plunge into chapter books but still like colorful pictures.

STEP INTO READING® is designed to give every child a successful reading experience. The grade levels are only guides. Children can progress through the steps at their own speed, developing confidence in their reading, no matter what their grade.

Remember, a lifetime love of reading starts with a single step!

To GK, who makes me happy
—B.B.
To BB, my wonderful wife
—G.K.
For happy birthdays—always!
—D.B.

Text copyright © 2001 by Barbara Bottner and Gerald Kruglik. Illustrations copyright © 2001 by Denise Brunkus/Silverpin Studio. All rights reserved under International and Pan-American Copyright Conventions. Published in the United States by Random House Children's Books, a division of Random House, Inc., New York, and simultaneously in Canada by Random House of Canada Limited, Toronto. Originally published by Golden Books, an imprint of Random House Children's Books, a division of Random House, Inc., New York, in 2001.

www.stepintoreading.com

Educators and librarians, for a variety of teaching tools, visit us at www.randomhouse.com/teachers

Library of Congress Cataloging-in-Publication Data
Bottner, Barbara.
It's not Marsha's birthday / by Barbara Bottner and Gerald Kruglik ; illustrated by Denise Brunkus.
   p.   cm. — (Step into reading. A step 3 book)
SUMMARY: Lulu wants her birthday to be special and she does not want to share it with her baby sister, so she decides to spend it at the zoo with a gorilla who is also turning eight.
ISBN 0-307-26333-9 (trade) — ISBN 0-307-46333-8 (lib. bdg.)
[1. Birthdays—Fiction.   2. Sisters—Fiction.   3. Zoos—Fiction.   4. Gorillas—Fiction.]
I. Kruglik, Gerald.   II. Brunkus, Denise, ill.   III. Title.   IV. Series: Step into reading. Step 3 book.
PZ7.B6586   It   2004   [E]—dc21   2002015238

Printed in the United States of America   12 11 10 9 8 7 6 5 4 3
First Random House Edition

STEP INTO READING, RANDOM HOUSE, and the Random House colophon are registered trademarks of Random House, Inc.

STEP INTO READING®

STEP 3

It's Not Marsha's Birthday

by Barbara Bottner and Gerald Kruglik
illustrated by Denise Brunkus

Random House 🏠 New York

"It's almost my birthday,"
Lulu said to Marsha.
"In one week I'll be eight.
Can you say *Happy Birthday, Lulu*?"
"Loo-loo!" Marsha said.

"No, say *Happy Birthday, Lulu*,"
said Lulu.

"Loo-loo!" Marsha said again.

"Oh, never mind," sighed Lulu.

"Can I have a party?"
Lulu asked her dad.
"I'll invite Murphy and Jackson."
"Of course," said Lulu's dad.
"And Marsha will be there, too."

"Marsha!" said Lulu.

"Who cares about Marsha!
I want a big party with clowns
and a puppet show.
And a magician and acrobats.
I want to be on TV, too!"

"Lulu, I don't think we can do all that,"
said her mom.
"But I will bake you a special cake."
Lulu frowned and stomped
into the kitchen.

On the kitchen table,
the newspaper was turned
to a picture of a gorilla.
Lulu read the headline.
"Samoo Turns Eight Next Week."

"Wow!" thought Lulu.

"I bet Samoo will have a big party
with clowns and a puppet show.
And a magician and acrobats.
I'm sure he'll be on TV, too."
Suddenly, Lulu had an idea.
She ran back into the other room.

"I know what I want to do
for my birthday," said Lulu.

"I want to see Samoo."

"Is Samoo a new friend
from school?" asked her mom.

"No! Samoo is a gorilla.
He lives in the zoo,
and he is going to be eight, too,"
said Lulu.

She showed her parents the picture.

"What a great idea!" said Lulu's dad.

"Let's go to the zoo!"

"Yay!" yelled Lulu.

"Ssseal!" said Marsha.

She held up her stuffed animal.

"That's right, Marsha," said her dad.

"There are seals at the zoo, too.

So both my girls will be happy."

"Who cares if Marsha is happy?"

grumbled Lulu.

"It's not Marsha's birthday!

It's mine!"

That night, Lulu spread out
a map of the zoo on her bed.
She saw that the seals
were on the way to the gorillas.
Everything was on the way
to the gorillas.
They were the very last stop
on the trail.

Lulu stared at the picture of Samoo.
He had a hairy body, large eyes,
and a big mouth.
Lulu thought she would much rather
have a gorilla than a baby sister.

Lulu counted the days to her birthday.
When it finally came, she put on
her brightest yellow sweater.
She didn't want Samoo to miss her.

After breakfast her dad
gave her a red balloon.
He also tied one to Marsha's stroller.
"So I can always spot my girls," he said.

"When you get home,
your birthday cake will be ready,"
said Lulu's mom.
She kissed Lulu.
But she hugged Marsha forever!
Everyone always loved Marsha.
Even on *Lulu's* birthday!

Lulu's father picked up
Murphy and Jackson.
Lulu waited for them
to say Happy Birthday.
But instead Murphy said,
"Let's see the lions!"
"They're my favorite," said Jackson.
"Ssseal!" giggled Marsha.
"Listen, everybody!" said Lulu.
"We're going to see the gorillas first."
"But the gorillas just sit there!"
said Murphy.
"They are so boring!" said Jackson.
Lulu groaned.

As they entered the zoo,
they saw a sign:

Lion Feeding
at 3 pm

"It's almost time," said Jackson.
"Let's go!"
"If I knew you were going
to be like this," yelled Lulu,
"I would not have invited you."

"Lulu, it's okay," said her dad.

"We will have time to see the gorillas."

Lulu shut her eyes while
the zookeeper fed the hungry lions.
"Lulu, did you see them gobble up
the meat?" asked Murphy.
"Yuck!" said Lulu.

"Lions have to eat, too," said her dad.

"You care too much about the lions and not enough about my birthday!" said Lulu.

Lulu's dad sighed.

The next stop was the seal pool.
"We promised Marsha we'd
see the seals," said Lulu's dad.
"It will only take a few minutes."
"This is so wrong!" Lulu grumbled.
"It's not Marsha's birthday!"

Inside, Lulu marched up

to the biggest seal.

She made the most awful face she could.

The next thing she knew,

she was dripping wet.

Everyone started laughing.

"This is not funny," said Lulu.

"I feel like an egg yolk!"

Lulu didn't like seals.

And she didn't like being laughed at.

Lulu ran outside.

"I'm all wet," grumbled Lulu.

She tried to dry off her sweater—

and her balloon flew away!

She chased after it.

It flew higher and higher into the sky.

Then it was gone.

Lulu looked around.

She didn't see her dad.

How would he find her

without her red balloon?

Lulu was scared.

She didn't know what to do.

Suddenly, she heard a strange noise.

It sounded like—a gorilla!

Of course!

Samoo's party.

He must be waiting for her!

GORILLAS →

Lulu ran into the gorilla house.

It didn't look like there was a party.

Where were the clowns and the puppets?

And the magician and the acrobats?

Where were the TV cameras?

Was she too late?

Then Lulu saw a very large gorilla.

It was Samoo.

Nobody was paying attention to him.

"Poor Samoo," said Lulu.

"Everyone forgot your birthday.

Everyone but me!"

Samoo stared at Lulu.

"Happy Birthday!" Lulu said.

"It's my birthday, too."

She waved at Samoo.

Samoo lifted his hand.

Was he waving back?

Lulu wasn't sure.

She moved closer.

"Don't feel bad," said Lulu.

She put her chin in her hands.

Samoo wrapped his big hands

around his chin, too.

"I came to see you," Lulu told Samoo.

Lulu tickled her stomach.

Samoo did the same.

Lulu leaned toward Samoo
and threw him a kiss.
Samoo threw a kiss back to Lulu.
Lulu smiled.

Lulu wished that Marsha
and the others could see
how much Samoo loved her.

Suddenly, she heard a voice.

"Loo-loo!"

Then she saw a red balloon.

It was Marsha.

"Over here!" called Lulu.

"You shouldn't have run off,"

said Lulu's dad.

"We were so worried!"

"I'm sorry," said Lulu.

"But watch this!"

Lulu pounded her chest.

So did Samoo.

"Cool!" said Jackson.

"And you said gorillas were boring!"
said Murphy.

The boys jumped up and down.

But Samoo only yawned.

"Samoo really likes you, Lulu,"
said her dad.

"He *loves* me," said Lulu.

"Me, too!" Marsha said.

Marsha waved her hand.

But Samoo did not move.

Marsha's head drooped.

"OK, everyone," said her dad.

"It's time to go home."

"Do we really have to?" asked Lulu.

"Your mom is waiting

at home with your cake.

Don't you want us to sing

Happy Birthday, Lulu?" asked her dad.

"Happy Birthday, Loo-loo," said Marsha.

"You finally said it!" cried Lulu.

Lulu took Marsha's hand.

They waved to Samoo.

This time Samoo waved back.

Marsha clapped and hugged Lulu.

She gave Lulu her red balloon.

"Samoo, this is my
baby sister!" said Lulu.

"She loves me, too!"